WEATHER TECH
A First Look

KATIE PETERS

GRL Consultant, Diane Craig, Certified Literacy Specialist

Lerner Publications ◆ Minneapolis

TABLE OF CONTENTS

Weather Tech 4

Weather Tech

People study the
weather.
They use many tools.

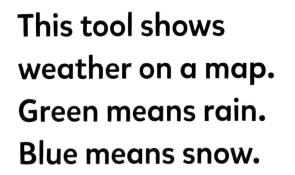

This tool shows
weather on a map.
Green means rain.
Blue means snow.

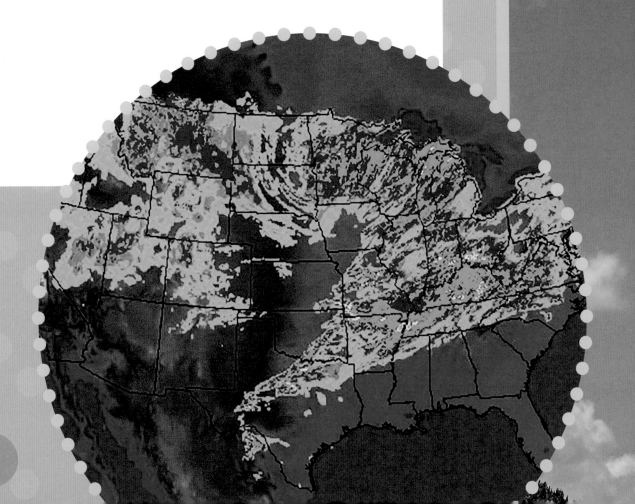

radar

People put machines up into outer space. They tell us about weather on Earth.

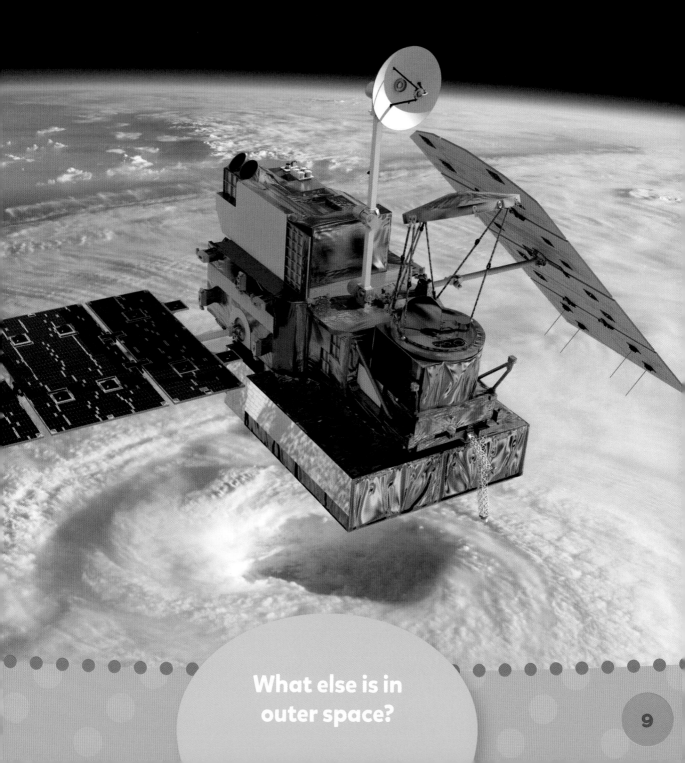

What else is in outer space?

The machines take pictures of Earth. The pictures show where storms are.

Weather balloons tell us about weather too.

weather balloon

They float far above
the ground.

This tool shows how hot or cold it is.

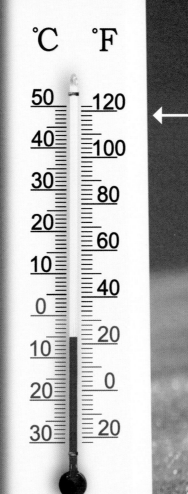

°C   °F

50   120

40   100

30   80

20   60

10   40

0   20

10   0

20   20

30   20

thermometer

Some tools show how
fast the wind is going.

Others show which
way it is going.

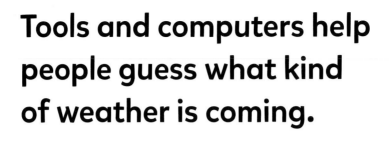

Tools and computers help people guess what kind of weather is coming.

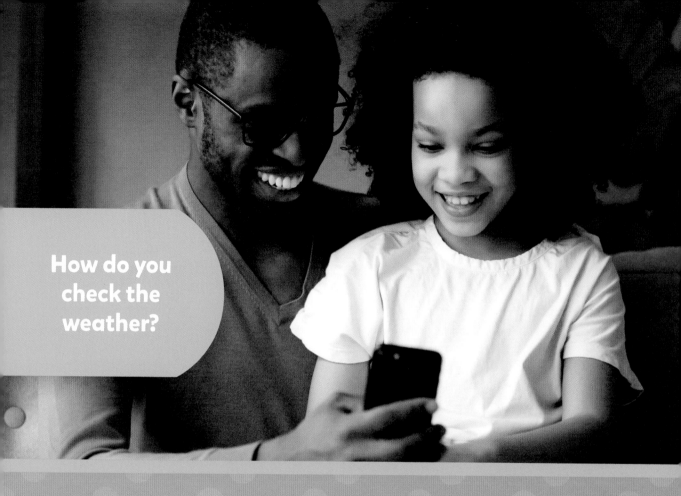

How do you check the weather?

People check the weather with phones and computers.

It will be sunny tomorrow!

You Connect!

What is something you like about weather tech?

What kinds of weather tech have you seen?

How do you find out about the weather?

STEM Snapshot

Encourage students to think and ask questions like a scientist! Ask the reader:

What is something you learned about weather tech?

What is something you noticed about weather tech in the pictures in this book?

What is something you still don't know about weather tech?

Photo Glossary

balloon

computer

machine

phone

Learn More

Nelson, Penelope S. *Forecasting Weather*. Minneapolis: Abdo, 2019.

Ralston, Fraser, and Judith Ralston. *What's the Weather? Clouds, Climate, and Global Warming*. New York: DK, 2021.

Rustad, Martha E. H. *Let's Notice Weather Patterns*. Minneapolis: Lerner Publications, 2022.

Index

Photo Acknowledgments

The images in this book are used with the permission of: © Frame Stock Footage/Shutterstock Images, pp. 4–5; © Donna Chance Hall/Shutterstock Images, pp. 6–7; © NOAA National Weather Service/Wikimedia Commons, p. 6; © Britt Griswold/Flickr, pp. 8–9, 23; © Zenobillis/Shutterstock Images, pp. 10–11; © Edward Haylan/Shutterstock Images, pp. 12–13, 23; © Tomas Ragina/Shutterstock Images, pp. 14–15; © Petty Officer 3rd Class Sean Lynch/Public Domain, p. 16; © Praisaeng/Shutterstock Images, p. 17; © Burlingham/Adobe Stock, pp. 18, 23; © fizkes/Shutterstock Images, pp. 19, 23; © CandyRetriever/Shutterstock Images, p. 20.

Cover Photograph: © Tomas Ragina/Adobe Stock

Design Elements: © Mighty Media, Inc.

Copyright © 2024 by Lerner Publishing Group, Inc.

Lerner Publications Company
An imprint of Lerner Publishing Group, Inc.
241 First Avenue North
Minneapolis, MN 55401 USA

For reading levels and more information, look up this title at www.lernerbooks.com.

Main body text set in Mikado a Medium.
Typeface provided by Hannes von Doehren.

Library of Congress Cataloging-in-Publication Data

Names: Peters, Katie, author.
Title: Weather tech : a first look / Katie Peters.
Description: Minneapolis : Lerner Publications, 2024. | Series: Read about weather (read for a better world) | Includes bibliographical references and index. | Audience: Ages 5–8 | Audience: Grades K–1 | Summary: "There are many different tools that help us measure and predict the weather. With leveled text and full-color photographs, young readers will enjoy seeing the world of weather tech"—Provided by publisher.
Identifiers: LCCN 2023005909 (print) | LCCN 2023005910 (ebook) | ISBN 9798765608814 (library binding) | ISBN 9798765616864 (epub)
Subjects: LCSH: Weather forecasting—Technique—Juvenile literature. | BISAC: JUVENILE NONFICTION / Science & Nature / Earth Sciences / Weather
Classification: LCC QC995.48 .P48 2024 (print) | LCC QC995.48 (ebook) | DDC 551.63—dc23/eng20230714

LC record available at https://lccn.loc.gov/2023005909
LC ebook record available at https://lccn.loc.gov/2023005910

Manufactured in the United States of America
1 – CG – 12/15/23